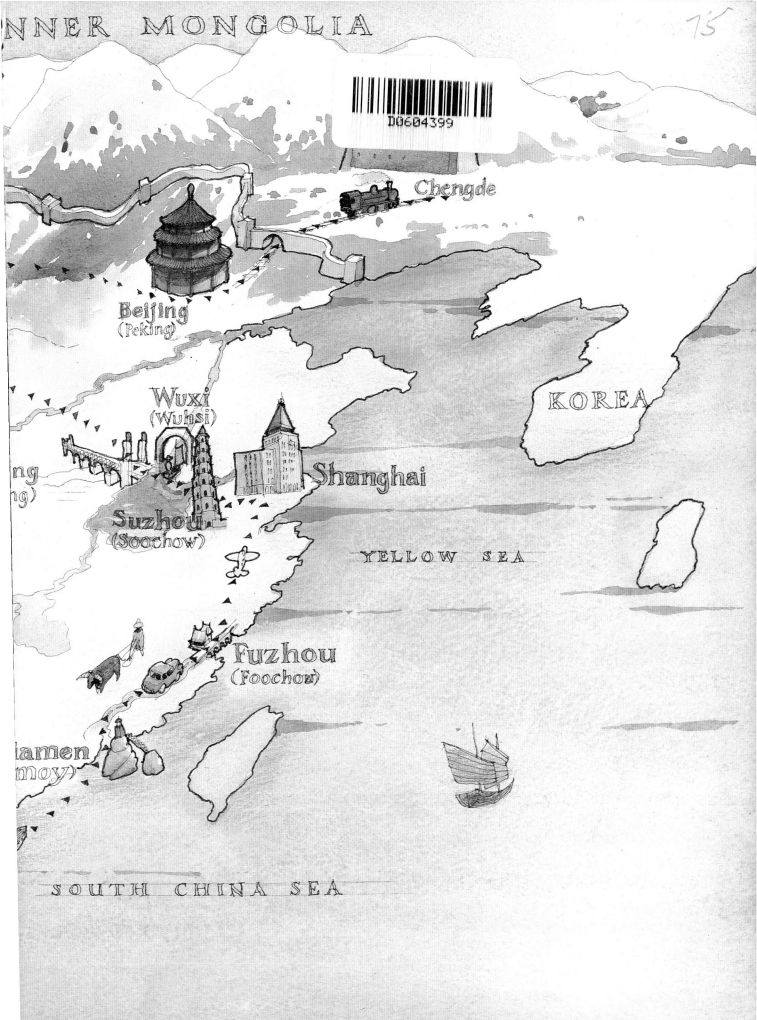

INNER MONGOLIA

75

Chengde

Beijing
(Peking)

Wuxi
(Wuhsi)

ng
g)

Suzhou
(Soochow)

Shanghai

KOREA

YELLOW SEA

Fuzhou
(Foochow)

iamen
moy)

SOUTH CHINA SEA

CHINA
JOURNEY

CHINA JOURNEY

MEREHURST PRESS
LONDON

Published 1988 by Merehurst Press
5 Great James Street, London WC1N 3DA

© Amanuensis Books Limited 1988

By arrangement with Amanuensis Books Limited

ISBN 1 85391 021 X

This book was designed and produced by
Amanuensis Books Limited
12 Station Road
Didcot
Oxfordshire OX11 7LN

Reproduction by Eclipse Litho Ltd

Printed and bound in Spain by Graficas Reunidas SA

Contents

The sketches

The water colour sketches in this book were developed from the sketch books which I filled on the journey. We took 20 books with us but it was soon obvious that I was carrying a lot of dead weight since it took a lot longer to finish 44 sides of book than I had imagined.

Train journeys became my favourite method of travel for they not only provided a constant change of subject but also a good sized flat table with excellent light and a reasonably smooth ride. I also found that green tea makes perfectly adequate mixing water if you can live with the faint green tinge that it gives your picture.

Most of the original writing was done in hotel bedrooms by the light of a 20 watt bulb high in the ceiling but it was most comfortable to work on restaurant tables over meals — sometimes finding the subjects on the other tables. For that kind of work I found that the easiest method was to use a .5 or a .35 technical drawing pen loaded with a waterproof sepia drawing ink for both drawing and writing. These produce a fairly thick line but at least they don't clog too often. In the evening it was usually a matter of spreading a few dabs from the water colour tubes onto the rim of the basin or the edge of the loo and applying a light wash.

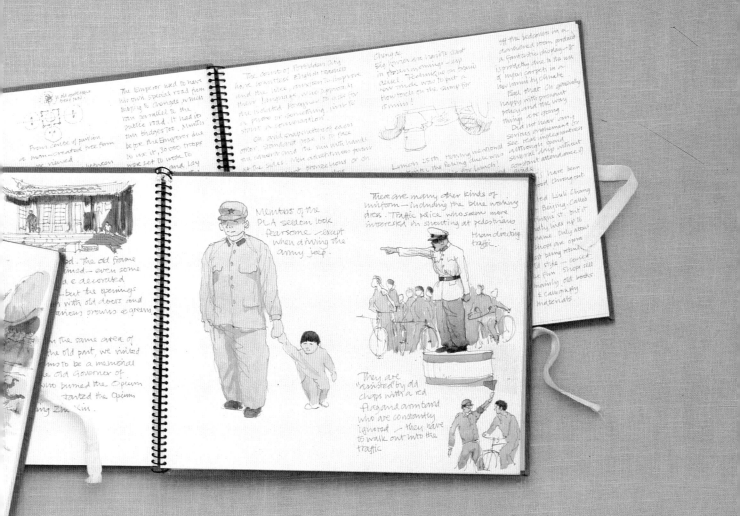

Carol took many photographs which I have sometimes used as a basis for the sketches. They are not ideal, however, as they tend to contain too much detail in which the wrong things become emphasised. I felt it was important to record my reaction to the events of the day as soon as possible before they became confused or too considered. Most of the time I have tried to keep away from the realities of the guide books and stick to my personal first impressions but some facts have had to be included to keep things in perspective.

It was my original intention to see if anyone was interested in publishing the sketch books as they stood. They have the advantage of being immediate even if they are a bit chaotic. Later it seemed a good idea to make a series of sketches and notes which could be printed together in a book but the project would have proved too expensive for a publisher. If on the other hand I could write 20,000 words of text to go with the sketches and agree to some of them being in black and white then maybe something could be worked out...

China Journey

Lantau Island

In the mid-60s, Carol and I decided that we wanted to visit China. We had worked in Hong Kong alongside six million Chinese and lived under the daily influence of our gigantic neighbour, eating food brought in from Guangzhou and drinking water pumped from Sum Chun, so it was not surprising that we were curious to see what lay beyond the border and the barbed wire fences.

At that time a visa application was not easy and you had to be ready to go when it came through. By the time ours was ready the Red Guards were creating havoc so we agreed to postpone the journey for a while. It was a long postponement because it was not until we were about to leave Hong Kong for good that we tried again. By this time, tourist travel in China had become much easier to arrange, and many of her cities were open to visitors.

To keep our timetable as loose as we could, we decided to travel alone — or as alone as the Chinese would permit us to be. Rumour had it that all private tourists were constantly lead by their guide. Although it was clear that our journey would take us to some of the major tourist areas, we also wanted to visit the less well-known places where we hoped to avoid the crowds and see the real China.

I have visited cities, admired priceless treasure only to find later that they become a confused jumble of images. This time it was going to be different. We would read about the places and their history beforehand and to make sure we really did look, I would sketch and makes notes and Carol would take photographs. If the photos turned out well I would use them to make further sketches. I did think there was a possibility that the whole lot could be made into a book, but if nothing else, the discipline would ensure that we thought about and recorded what we saw instead of just staring like we do at television.

Our journey really started on Lantau Island in Hong Kong, where we had been invited to stay by two of our friends, Pat and 'Nig' Nigel. They were going away for a few weeks and thought that we might like to make use of their house with its secluded garden to do our studying. It is in a stunning position on top of a hill facing due south, ideal for anyone relaxing or working quietly.

Livestock at the Nigel's included a plague of large woodland spiders, real monsters with legspans of eight or nine inches and webs some five foot across. They have huge poison fangs which can give a human a nasty bite. Pat took us on a tour of the wooded terrace leading the way along the lesser used paths. Every few yards she would leap into the air and deliver an overhead

smash with her walking stick at one of these giant woodland spiders sitting in the middle of its cobweb slung between the trees. She was deadly accurate and anyone who has had their face wrapped in one of these tough, sticky webs can understand her reasons. However, I did ponder that should she miss, a large angry spider would drop on top of her from a great height.

Pat was not really anti-spider. She was particularly fond of a large, hairy beast which she said was the family pet. It lived under the rim of the lavatory in the guest loo. No amount of flushing could dislodge it. When I think of the times I used the loo before I knew of its existence, I get a strange tickling sensation.

China Journey

Nig did give us one warning before he left and that was to knock the heel of each shoe before putting it on because centipedes like to curl up in the warm leather. The first morning on our own I lifted up the newspaper left on the terrace from the previous night, and there was the biggest centipede we had ever seen. Panic ensued. We rushed about shouting, but eventually I managed to trap it under a glass topped table and measure it before letting it go. It was ten and half inches long.

A couple of frogs lived in the swimming pool skimmers and there was a lizard living in the drinks refrigerator at the pool — seldom seen, but it always left its mark. Geckos abounded, and watching them catch insects could be as hypnotic as watching the television. I have never understood how the gecko can hold on upside down with such tiny feet.

That autumn in Lantau was lazily beautiful. We read about China, practised sketching among the boats of the island villages, visited the early morning fish markets and sat looking out at the South China Sea. The highlight of most evenings was a visit to the Tong Fuk Hilton, more often known as Fuk's, for a curry or local dish eaten in the area between the rusting remains of a van and stacks of beer crates. Here, under the palm trees, one could chat to the other customers — a Chinese hiker, a German banker, an off-duty policeman, a group of Gurkha soldiers, even a man who claimed to be a White Russian refugee.

Eventually the time came for us to pack our bags with our warmest clothes, load in a few books, a jar of instant coffee, sketchbooks, sewing kit, toilet paper, dysentery pills — all the things a tourist carries when he doesn't quite know what he is getting himself into.

We took the slow drive down to the ferry. The traffic on South Lantau Road is often held up by bullock carts. In fact, my last memory of Lantau was of a large water buffalo standing patiently by the side of the road while an old woman tied on shoes cut from an inner tube to stop its hooves slipping on the steep hill.

Tai-O fishing village scene.

China Journey

Hong Kong to Xiamen

At first it seemed a good idea to go to China by ferry instead of flying. I imagined standing on the deck of the steamer to Xiamen admiring the fishing junks and the sights of the China coast. I did have some reservations about being seasick and was relieved to find that the *New Jimei* was fairly large and ship-sized rather than boat-sized.

Over the side hung the gangway lined from top to bottom with stewards. They looked much like stewards anywhere except that the girls were dressed in grey uniforms, white collars and black ties. They fitted like a sack. I thought they were waiting to take our bags, but as each passenger crossed from the raft onto the swaying gangway, the stewards just smiled and patted the suitcases as they passed. Maybe it had something to do with the dignity of labour.

The *New Jimei* turned out to be the repainted *Norwegian Princess* which is why it looked much the same as any other passenger ship. On the deck the steel was almost rusted through. I suppose I was a little disappointed that the ship was so ordinary, so Scandinavian. It had very little about it that looked Chinese apart from the colour scheme of red, yellow and green. Although the ship was Western, its occupants were clearly not. We were unused to the thermos flasks of hot water, jelly-green flip-flops in the cabin for our use, and pot plants all over the deck. We looked everywhere in the cabin for the key until we were told that a key was quite unnecessary. There was no crime in China.

Hong Kong to Xiamen

We had lived in Hong Kong for 20 years, but when we looked at the city from six storeys up in the middle of the harbour, it looked totally different, rather like an architect's scale model. As we sailed slowly out of the crowded water, buildings which were so familiar from the land took on a completely new appearance.

It was a stunning day, very clear and sunny, typical November weather. I had not realized just how big Hong Kong was until we had sailed the length of the harbour. First came the glossy hotels, The Regent with its horizontal stripes, then the office blocks with their glass curtain walls. These gradually gave way to high-rise warehouses and when they had gone there was nothing but the squatter huts clinging to the hillsides, the occupants hoping they would still be there after the next typhoon.

Squatter huts cling to Hong Kong's hillsides.

17

'New Jimei'

Apart from the occasional sea-going junk set against the low, rolling hills, there was little happening out to sea and the coast proved to be almost empty. On board the ship was quiet except for announcements in Mandarin over the tannoy. It turned out that they were announcing lunch — so we missed that. A steward was sent to fetch us for dinner.

Dinner was an interesting experience for us and an entertaining one for the others at our table. The food was quite different from anything we had eaten in Hong Kong and some of the slippery things were hard to keep in the chopsticks, but we enjoyed the meal. At breakfast I wanted to take a photo, but the waiter came and stood over me. I still took the picture. We had nuts and a sort of dried pork which looked like a heap of hair. After dunking it in a kind of rice gruel it tasted quite good.

Hong Kong to Xiamen

The saloon acted as the meeting place on the ship. All of the seats were full and on the sofas people were sleeping or drinking tea. At the bar I asked for a whiskey and water. The barman explained that there was no cold water, only boiling water, so I would have to wait until the ice had cooled it down sufficiently.

Here we met some of the English speaking passengers — one woman was going to see her relatives for the first time in 40 years. A Hong Kong man hoped to sell Taiwanese shoe machinery to the Chinese. A young pale-face girl (who I took to be a hooker) quietly said she and her large man friend were visiting a conference on business. A very overweight Hawaiian Chinese girl was on her way to visit her parents and meet the man they had arranged for her to marry. When we explained what we were doing, many were surprised that foreigners should want to start a visit to their country in the town of Xiamen.

Music woke us in the morning, starting with Bach, changing to a light music selection by mid-morning which later gave way to pop. As we approached the port of Xiamen and prepared to line up for passport checks, Peking Opera was blasting at full volume from the tannoy.

Lighthouse at the entrance to Xiamen harbour.

Xiamen

In the early morning mist the *New Jimei* quietly eased its way along the coast towards Xiamen harbour. We passed the lighthouse, precariously perched on top of boulders, then swept into the muddy waters of the harbour to begin the slow journey upriver to our berth. There was an air of excitement on deck. Returning residents pointed out landmarks to people like ourselves who were visiting for the first time. Others stood quietly.

On the left bank I caught glimpses of buildings through the trees. One of the passengers pointed out a fine building of colonnaded stone with a red tile dome set high in landscaped gardens. He explained with pride that the building had once been part of the university, but had been turned into an electronics factory. The right bank was a complete contrast. Sheds, brick buildings, cranes and shipyards sprawled out from the docks housing traditional sea-going junks, trawlers, barges and tugs. We had no wish to be mistaken for spies, so we gave the menacing navy ships only a passing glance. The river was alive with small boats, some powered along at speed by smoky outboard motors others heavily laden and rowed deftly across the river with a single oar.

Xiamen

We eased our way into the berth and the anchor chain clattered over the side. Waiting at the foot of the gangway was an attractive young Chinese dressed in the same kind of bright clothes found in Hong Kong. She introduced herself in precise English, enquired if we had enjoyed the voyage, then set off at a brisk pace for the customs shed. This was Choi, the English-speaking guide we had asked for.

Customs clearance is always tedious. The customs woman needed to make a note of all items of value which we carried. This seemed to mean everything worth more than a few pounds, so although she remained cheerful and polite, it took a rather long time.

The bank stood in one corner of the cavernous shed. We handed over our bundle of foreign notes. Before exchanging them for the tourist cash known as yuan, the girl behind the ornate iron grill held every single note up against a bare bulb before passing it over to her neighbour who repeated the operation in every painstaking detail.

Choi herded us out of the shed, fought her way across the road through the locked mass of cyclists and into a lace-curtained car. The driver took on the challenge of the cyclists with determination and a great deal of hooting, pressing the car through the throng without hitting anyone. After 15 minutes of cut and thrust we arrived at the hotel to leave our bags. As we neared the doors to the lobby, a large tricycle carrying a pair of heavily built men and about 20 electric fans, beat us to it and pedalled smoothly across the marble lobby and out the other end scattering hotel residents in every direction.

From the hotel window I looked out over the roofs of the old town which swept away below me in a random, directionless pattern. Out of this waving sea of tiles towered majestic trees. This was the area I wanted to visit, but Choi had other ideas.

Our first meal on Chinese soil was in the Chinese Overseas Club. It did not seem to be a club in any sense of the word as I understood it. The rooms were vast whitewashed halls with brown tiled floors. Ornament was non-existent, no pictures decorated the walls and the furniture was sparse and basic. Although it was a little after noon when one would expect the club to be at its busiest, the atmosphere was quiet and deserted. One or two diners still sat at their tables, but they paid no attention to us.

After lunch we set out to see Xiamen. The streets were lined with four-storey shop-houses exactly like the old streets in Hong Kong which I knew so well. The upper floors projected over the pavement forming an arcade for the shops below. Every shop was open-fronted and gloomy — the gloom becoming deeper as you ventured further into the recesses, past rows of mahogany shelves

The Xiamen waterfront is packed with a variety of small craft — mostly traditional fishing junks.

Xiamen

roftops of the Old City
of Xiamen

and drawers and glass cases. Many of the shops were herbalists, stocking unmentionable objects pickled in alcohol in glass jars, brightly-coloured powders and row upon row of ready-mixed medicines.

Outside in the sunlight a group of three young men was trying to manhandle a dark red velvet sofa and armchairs into one of the shops. Two struggled with the armchair while the third stretched out and dozed on the sofa at the side of the road. Choi did not like the idea of us going through the narrow passages between the shop-houses. That was the way into the Old City. She told us frankly that she felt it did not represent today's China and she was sure we would prefer to visit the newer parts where the skills of China's engineers and artisans could be fully appreciated. We agreed — for the moment.

A dusty, grey pall hung over these new suburbs. They were a grey, dreary mess of concrete, mud and rubble, utterly unattractive. Grey concrete roads enclosed areas of grey uneven earth and anything that was not made of solid concrete was covered in grey concrete plaster.

We were persuaded to look at a new office building, then half finished, and although we tried to look interested our hearts were not in it. After half an hour we felt that we could leave without offending Choi and head for something more picturesque. In the middle of this unappealing scene we would catch a glimpse of an exquisite piece of carving or some hidden, fascinating building.

The elegant, long boat-roof of the dentist's house suddenly appeared through a gap in the wall. We walked towards it through a derelict garden strewn with headless stone statues of minor officials. A hairy black pig rooted amongst them for food. We passed under the intricately carved doorway into the courtyard beyond. Chickens and dogs added their contribution to the talking and shouting. We joined a family group and watched with morbid curiosity as the dentist operated.

Among the headless statues a black, hairy pig rooted for food.

Xiamen

His surgery was open to the courtyard and the patient sat facing the light and the onlookers. Behind him was a picture of Lenin and below that was a basin supporting a tray loaded with several stainless steel instruments. I was disappointed not to see an acupuncture needle in sight. The dentist's performance was impressive, the patient's attitude suprisingly relaxed. The treadle-operated drill moved in and out of his open jaws, going in with a high-pitched whine and coming out droning slowly, whereupon the dentist pedalled energetically for a few seconds to pick the speed up before advancing on the open mouth once more.

By this time Choi was beginning to unwind, so we tactfully pointed out that although we were impressed by the city's latest achievements, we would like to see more of the old parts and the people who lived there. It was obvious that this was a part of the city she seldom, if ever, visited. However, she agreed to come with us.

Once inside the narrow alleyways the sun was shut out by overhanging eaves. Finding the way depended on your sense of direction which soon became confused. The lane meandered on, occasionally widening out to ten feet then narrowing to the more normal four or five. On either side the stuccoed walls of the houses and courtyards were relieved only by narrow entrances and tiny windows.

Choi spoke to an old woman who was brushing the courtyard. Her face lit up when she was asked if she would mind showing us her house. We were invited inside where the change in atmosphere was remarkable. Outside it had felt dark and threatening, but inside the courtyard it was light and hospitable. A large tree grew in the yard. Bamboo poles were attached to it and each was draped with washing hung on plastic coat hangers. In one corner stood an ancient pump which seemed to be the sole source of water for the house.

Inside the house everything was clean, but broken furniture, tools, bundles and anything which might conceivably come in useful one day was heaped in piles against every wall. The tiny clear space in the middle housed a few pieces of furniture, unpainted, repaired and very basic. The sole concessions to decoration were three sepia photographs and a number of pot plants.

A few miles out of town lies the thousand-year-old South Putuo Temple. The buildings could have been taken from a Chinese picture book. Great sweeping roofs, ornate filigreed eaves, brightly painted calligraphy on decorative friezes and a fantastically ornate pagoda.

Looking around with the delight of schoolboys on an outing was a group of 20 customs officers. I took out my pen and started

China Journey

South Putuo Temple with its exotic roofs and curly finials.

to sketch them. One came over and made clear signs that I should stick to drawing the pagoda and leave him and his friends out of it or things could become rather serious. Suddenly I could see things his way, so we went over to the pagoda instead.

I was surprised that in spite of the government's attitude to religion, there appeared to be some freedom of worship, but when I looked around it seemed to rely entirely on women and monks. Inside the pagoda the approach to worship was different from any we had known — there was a casual, unaffected attitude towards the ceremony and the women lit joss sticks, threw prayer sticks in the air, talked, laughed and shouted to each other.

The main temple stood beyond the pagoda. We went in and were astonished at the scene that met us. Stretching high into the gloom of the wooden roof beams were three gigantic, wooden Buddhist figures gazing down at us. Incense smoke wreathed upwards, filling the roof space with a purple mist through which hung long prayer banners. The sound of chanting came from a door at the side. It grew louder as a column of monks filed in, their heads bowed, their robes of saffron, black and brown swaying as they walked to the beating of the gong. The monks heads were shaven and many of them had a ring of circular scars left from the initiation ceremony in which lighted candles were placed on their heads and allowed to burn down to the scalp. The serpentine line of monks wound around the floor then they stepped between the saffron cushions and knelt, chanting without a break. The hypnotic rhythm and smell of incense seemed to fill the temple. We stood and watched the ceremony in silence and when it was over, walked out into the sun.

South Putuo Temple. An intensely moving and
powerful ceremony.

China Journey

The next day we took a short ferry ride to Gulanyu (the Garden of the Sea), a picturesque area dominated by a massive rock known as Sunset Peak. The route up to the Peak was steep and wound through streets of lovely houses surrounded by masses of flowers and palm trees. Eventually the road changed to a wonderful flight of steps with irregular stones which wound up between the boulders in such a way as to appear completely natural. Twenty-foot high characters and Chinese couplets were carved into the smooth surface of the giant stones in the tradition of Chinese landscape design.

From the top of the peak I looked down on the entire city laid out in a pattern of red tiled roofs, green trees and purple patches of bougainvillaea. Then I spotted something which still makes my palms sweat when I think of it — a couple of young men stepped casually over the safety railings onto the curved dome of rock with nothing between them and a 200 foot drop except their nerve and the friction of their flip-flops.

Gulanyu is completely free of cars and bicycles which makes it an ideal place to study the architectural puzzles presented by the buildings. The outside influences were introduced when several hundred British soldiers and ships persuaded the Chinese to grant to British entrepreneurs the right to live and trade in the city. This Treaty of Nanking, like to many other 'Treaties' signed by the Chinese around this time, was a one-sided arrrangement. The cities became known as 'Treaty Ports'. Many of Gulanyu's major buildings show this strong European influence, but it is not always British. For instance, there is a white painted church at which worship appears to be permitted, which would not look out of place in nineteenth-century Germany. Some of the houses are very similar to the Portuguese terraces in Macau with flat arches and shuttered windows.

Carol asked if I had noticed that Choi had not only unwound, but she had been asking about European and American fashions. Also she had changed her clothes several times, sometimes over lunch, and she began to talk about her life. She was the daughter of an English language professor at the local university. She had not yet been out of China although she wanted to and she improved her English by listening to the radio. Her real ambition in life was to become a clothes designer. This would be very difficult for her in a provincial town where most of the population wore nothing but blue worksuits all the time, but whenever we passed a clothes stall, she would dash over to see if there was anything to suit her, then she would start to bargain.

Down by the sea was a dance hall. It was not very different from those found in English seaside towns not so many years ago complete with a lightweight plastic roof, concrete floor, moulded stacking chairs, red and green balloons and a five-piece band. Only the music was different. The band played foxtrots, tangos and old-fashioned waltzes. The dances were very popular according to Choi who said she went there once a week to learn how to do the foxtrot properly. She didn't think her father would object to her dancing even if he knew, because it closed at ten o'clock in the evening. A more traditional form of entertainment was the maze wall which had once been a part of the garden of a large house and now belonged to the public. It was a wall of rock into which dozens of holes had been cut, linked by stairways and paths which twisted in such a manner as to give no idea of whether you were going up or down. The spectators below could join in the fun by shouting instructions to the faces reappearing in the openings.

Carol tried it and managed to get completely lost. She had to be brought out by the caretaker, much to his amusement.

It is an attractive walk
down from the high rocks of
'Sunset Peak'!

At the bottom lies the beach
and a park which originally
belonged to a private house.

The garden is really a rock
structure with a few plants
and trees.

The 44 zig-zag bridge
confuses the evil spirits.

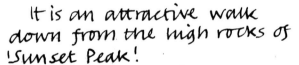

At one time, there
was a fort on the
highest point of
Gulangyu. The steps
leading up are varied
and feel very natural.

Xiamen to Fuzhou

We settled back to watch the scenery on the eight-hour journey to Fuzhou. Our Shanghai car was styled on the bulbous American designs of the late 50s, with a full complement of chrome. Official stickers decorated the windscreen at the front and the tiny window at the back was heavily curtained making it impossible for the driver to see behind. Not that the driver was concerned about what happened behind him. His ambition in life was to overtake everything in front, which he suceeded in doing. I would have preferred to have driven ourselves, but there are no hire cars and in any case, the signs are hard to read.

As we left the outskirts of Xiamen we saw why the town was so grey. The city was built of grey granite and surrounded by stone quarries. It was used everywhere even for fences where solid planks of granite were butted together to form an enclosure for pigs or cattle. Signposts, roads, houses, windows and even aqueducts were built from this expensive material. The form of local architecture was shaped by the granite as the columns and beams established the rhythm of the structure.

Further north the building material changed from granite to a reddish brick and clay. Kilns and entire brickworks appeared by the roadside. Some houses were built entirely out of large clay jars, plastered together — an original solution to the insulation problem but it must have been difficult to hang the pictures. Roof lines changed too, from the simple gable of the south to the complicated fluted gables of the villages nearer Fuzhou.

Seeing men on a treadmill came as something of a shock. In my mind it has always been associated with monotonous punishment, yet at the side of the road two men leaned on the rail of a

Granite signpost.

32

Roadside villages were often brightened with colourwash. Even the window surrounds were made of granite.

Some houses were built of jars.

Further North, brick kilns became common.

treadmill, chatting and joking as they walked endlessly to raise water from the irrigation ditch up to the fields.

Compared with the fields in Europe where one might only see the occasional farmworker, these commune fields were crowded with men and women hoeing, ploughing, ditch-digging, threshing and spreading nightsoil — I can't say why all these different tasks went on at the same time, but they did.

Generally the roads were good but sometimes they deteriorated into dusty tracks. As the roads became worse, our driver preferred to sound the horn rather than move the wheel to ward off oncoming lorries and suicidal cyclists. We stopped for lunch in a village with tree-lined, cobbled streets and white painted houses where we pulled into the parking lot of an office block. It had a large restaurant supervised by a woman dressed in the style of the Red Guards – blue suit, Mao cap and cropped hair. She looked daunting but she showed us to a table with a lace tablecloth and a bowl of flowers, then supervised serving the meal.

It was dark when we reached Fuzhou.

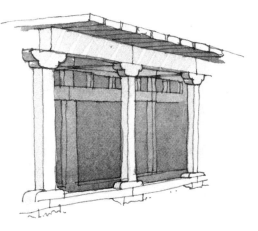

Granite is hard, attractive and it costs the earth — except in China! There it is used to enclose fields, build aqueducts and houses.

Xiamen to Fuzhou

Figures in the fields
of the village commune
moved slowly in the heat
of the day.

The massive water buffalo was not as friendly as it looked — much to the farmers amusement. Some of them are treated as pets.

Fuzhou

Fuzhou

Traffic signals in Fuzhou are rare, so control of busy intersections rests in the hands of traffic policemen armed with whistles. They are assisted by old men who also have whistles, armbands and red flags. Between them they control thousands of cyclists, pedestrians and a few cars and lorries. Unfortunately, it seems that whatever the assistant does, whether he whistles or waves his red flag, he is totally ignored. On the other hand the traffic policeman is always obeyed. We saw one cyclist miss his signal. Loud whistling brought the traffic to a halt and from his position on his stand the policeman berated the offender mercilessly while the rest of us watched.

Although Fuzhou is 2000 years old, it is not as popular with foreign tourists as it is with the Chinese themselves. However, it does have a huge industry making souvenirs and it seemed impolite not to visit some of them. We were glad we did.

The skill of the jade carvers was easy to appreciate and for us it was fun as they laughed while I sketched them at work. How much of the work was done in high quality jade and how much was in soap-stone and lesser jades I don't know but they started with a block of dull grey material onto which they splashed water to make it semi-transparent. This let them see inside the jade to understand the colours and planes. They say it then takes months to plan what is to be carved and how to approach it, and after more months of painstaking chipping and scraping, the final shape emerges. We watched the carving of a row of birds on a branch in which a deep red vein was exploited to give each bird a red head.

The lacquer factory was more in keeping with the image of the sweatshops of the East. The building was dreary with small windows and cramped conditions. It was uncomfortable to find that the atmosphere of the workplace had rubbed off on the workers and was not a happy one. The workers were sullen and uncommunicative. We were told this was because visitors might want to pirate their secrets.

The factory produces untold thousands of jars, trays and dishes in what is known as bodyless-laquerware. First a form is produced in what seems to be linen and plaster, then the lacquer coats are built up and repeatedly polished and relacquered. Up to 80 coats are used to create a mirror-finished object of the deepest black.

Young workers then trace on traditional Chinese scenes and outline them in gold for another to fill in the bright final colours. Most of this work is done against the window but on a dark day the only light comes from a bare bulb.

We had already seen clay carvers at work in Xiamen where the basic material was a rare clay which hardened without firing. Most of the finished objects were small, brightly painted figures from Chinese opera, but the studio of the master craftsman was dominated by a huge, half-finished eagle with a wingspan of eight feet. Without a doubt, these were highly skilled and talented craftsmen and I would have liked to take home some of their work. I asked if there were any good copies of the objects which are now in museums and galleries, but the answer was always that tourists preferred the kind of thing they had on display.

Jade carvers were a friendly crowd. They showed us how they exposed the colours buried deep in the stone.

In the lacquerware factory, the atmosphere was unfriendly — this may have reflected their concern that their working secrets may be stolen.

The unlacquered jars make interesting shapes in the sun.

The deep black lacquer is then painted in a traditional way.

Under the bridge passed heavily loaded barges, rowed by two oarsmen.

Before we left the lacquer factory, I asked for the meaning of the hundreds of characters on the red signboard near the entrance. This, it was explained, was a record of the number of children born to each member of the workforce. One of the workers had seven. Ideally each couple has only one child. When they have two, the government withdraws some of its privileges and financial support, and for three children they assess penalties. This policy is advertised on billboards throughout the city and some of them were even in English.

Across the broad river Min lies the old bridge, now heavily restored in concrete, and at its centre there is a small island on which stands a group of picturesque houses. Below the bridge on the muddy water, flat barges were rowed with single oars by pairs of rowers standing on the prow.

On the footpaths there were bicycle hawkers who repaired anything that belonged to a bike right there on the pavement. There were not only hawkers using the footpath as a workshop. We had even seen a machine operated by three men being used to comb kapok. At the far end of the bridge we found the main hawker market.

A beaten-up truck received a further beating from a heavy sledge hammer wielded by a mechanic. A crowd soon gathered.

China Journey

I had got it fixed in my mind that I could not leave without a pair of antique spectacles, the round kind in brass frames, so the hawker market seemed to be a good place to start looking. The woman selling specs could not believe that I really wanted such a thing. Instead she insisted that I try on a pair of the latest design. It was a bit like going into a chain store where they offered a selection of lenses but no eye test. You simply bought a pair which made the writing on the test page look the biggest. Her test card was in Chinese which made it simpler to turn down her offer in a friendly way and wander off to the clothes stalls.

A thing that struck us both about the clothes on sale and the clothes worn by the minority groups was that they were all very brightly coloured, not just reds and yellows, but flourescent colours which almost hurt the eyes. They made a startling contrast to the sombre shades of the working clothes of the majority of people.

The new guide, Guo, whom we met on our arrival in Fuzhou, had obviously decided that if we wanted we could be trusted out on our own so while he had a day off we made our way up to Drum Mountain. It is named after the noise made by rain on the rounded rocks. The Gushing Spring Monastery was built on its upper slopes and approached along a winding road between red walls. We never did find the spring, certainly nothing that could be called gushing, but as we were looking for it we suddenly found ourselves surrounded by schoolgirls. Possibly we were the first foreigners they had been able to touch. Anyhow, they touched our arms, peered into our eyes, pointed to our height and then drew back shuddering in mock horror. At least, I think it was mock.

Courtyard after courtyard stretched up the hill, each one surrounded by stepped roofs. After wandering through the open rooms we found ourselves down in the kitchens. They were really primitive and cold. In the open yard, hollowed out slabs of granite formed the laundry sinks with only a single hose supplying the cold water. The buckets and washing tubs were made of wood bound with steel straps and above us hung the washing on bamboo poles.

A girl who must have been about eighteen, walked barefoot across the cold stone flags, knelt at one of the stone basins and washed her long black hair. Behind her in the open kitchen two monks prepared the rice for the midday meal which they heaped into metal cauldrons housed in brick boilers. The kitchen could provide food for 2000 people but now only a few monks lived in the monastery.

The Keeper of the Scrolls was the image of a merry monk — plump, red-faced, with white stubble and a wide grin. He showed us the scrolls and books, some said to have been written in the

Gushing Spring Monastery. A girl washed her hair in the granite bowls.

blood of the writer. Many of them were very beautiful. His explanations in English, which he claimed to speak, were impossible to understand and the only words we caught were 'sanskrit' and 'Sri Lanka' which meant that most of our conversation was again in sign language with a few drawings thrown in. We were sorry to leave his company.

China Journey

Flanking the interior courtyard of the 'Gushing Spring Monastery' are the Drum and Bell pavilions – identical pagoda-like buildings with very up-swept eaves.

They were packed with Chinese sightseers.

The Keeper of the Scrolls was a plump, cheerful monk with a red nose, round specs and stubble.

He claimed that he spoke English but all we picked up was 'sanskrit' and 'Sri-Lanka'.

The scrolls were very beautiful.

Fuzhou to Shanghai

C.A.A.C. stands for 'China Airlines Always Cancel', or so we were told after waiting for two days for our flight to Shanghai. There was no point in trying to change airlines. There was only the state airline and after all, what did it matter? We simply had more time to spend looking at some of the things which we had either missed or wanted to see again.

Eventually, in the middle of a meal, we heard that there was a plane available. With no time to finish the meal, we grabbed our coats and headed for the airport to join the crowds in the departure hall for another long wait. Information about the flight was not easy to come by. The departures were written in chalk on a blackboard in Chinese and the announcements were all in Mandarin.

As we waited I noticed that the policeman sitting opposite us was wearing a pair of thick pyjamas under his uniform and wondered if he had forgotten to set his alarm that morning or whether he knew something about the temperature in Shanghai that we didn't.

Once in the air it was possible to appreciate why the coast of China is so crowded. Even from our modest height of about 15,000 feet the cultivated strip of flat land between the hills and the coast seemed very narrow indeed and once the hills had started there was nothing but more hills as far as the eye could see. Apart from the occasional twisting ribbon of a river, they were devoid of features, just barren grey folds.

We neared Shanghai and the sunlight faded. The grey hills turned to a deep purple as the rain began to fall. When we landed we knew why the policeman had kept his pyjamas on.

The 'Peace Hotel'. It is a time capsule of the 1920s.

Shanghai

For many years we had heard that life in Hong Kong was not a patch on life in Shanghai. No night club compared with the one in the Cathay Hotel where even now the same Henry Wu and the Syncopaters play the old tunes. The big houses in the English style had to be seen to be believed etc.

I already knew the history of many of the major buildings including the Cathay Hotel, from the records of the firm of architects I was with in Hong Kong. After the war their largest and most important office was the one in Shanghai and their photographs of the half-finished structures showed a world of coolies, rickshaws and white suits.

Shanghai

Today, the coolies and white suits have gone but the buildings remain largely unchanged by the passage of 60 years. When the hotel we stayed at was built in 1927 it was called the Cathay Hotel, but in the move to eradicate all signs of European influence its name was changed to the Peace Hotel.

Apart from a few plywood desks in the lobby, the interior looks as it must have done in the days before the war. Art deco mirrors, trimmed with bamboo, highlight the walls of the Piano Lounge. Lalique lamps from Paris hang from the lobby ceiling and everywhere there are sinuous plaster decorations. Of course, the front entrance has been closed off, and so have the front entrances of all the other major buildings on the waterfront. One of them now houses a butcher's stall, another a vegetable hawker.

To find out whether the real Henry Wu still played in the nightclub, we made our way past the bar which was still decorated in the original Scottish Baronial style to the source of the Glenn Miller music. Looking at the staid group on the bandstand, playing against the background of maroon velvet curtains and fairy lights, it was hard to believe that they could really be producing the big band sounds, yet the whole place was jumping and so were an American couple who were jiving. A great evening and where else can you have fun for only 85p for two?

Shanghai has a population of twelve million and most of them seemed to be in Nanjing Road going the opposite way from us. That might not have been too bad if it hadn't been for the storm which again turned day into night and brought out the umbrellas. The pavements had been widened into the road but even these did not create enough for the crowds, yet to step beyond the markers would have caused a multiple bicycle pile-up.

After wandering around all day, we tried to get back, but with no map and no knowledge of Mandarin, it was not easy. However, people were very friendly and had they known what we wanted they would have been only too happy to help, but it usually finished up with me wishing I had never asked and trying to back away without appearing impolite. In the end I drew a sketch of the Peace which was recognized instantly. Most gratifying.

Wang, our current guide, was a thin grey young man in a grey anorak who was not easy to see so we

China Journey

Nanjing Road on a wet evening.

kept losing him. He tended to shadow us rather than guide us, which was a problem in the crowds of Yu Gardens.

These gardens were the first real example of Chinese landscaping we had experienced, quite unlike anything we had imagined, mainly because they were so different from the gardens of Europe. The entrance to the gardens opened out from the narrow streets of the City onto a zig-zag bridge across a lake (the zig-zags were to confuse the evil spirits), then through a gate into the grassless, flowerless world of the city garden. Here, over 400 years ago, the designer brought together water and pavilions, bridges and paving patterns, poetry, puns, and calligraphy to make a garden for the mind as well as for the eyes.

It is really a very small garden but by clever use of space it has been made to appear much larger. The same spaces are used several times in different ways, sometimes to walk through, then to see through openings and then reflected under bridges. There is always something happening, from the moment the gardens open at eight in the morning to the time they close at six in the evening they give pleasure to a constant stream of people.

Shanghai

The Yu Garden is regarded as a landscaping masterpiece. On the summit of a man-made mountain, sits the 'Kuai Hall', like a scene from a Chinese painting, and with imagination one can see how the heavenly pavilion floats on the billowing clouds.

A screen inspired by the ancient religious symbol of the swastika.

Dragon-in-the-Clouds. A sinuous wall encloses part of the Yu Yuan and 7 marvellous dragons wave along the top of the wall.

Pools reflect the views beyond the walls.

Windows in the angled walls of parallel zig-zag corridors give surprising new views of the same scene. It is a deceptively simple yet effective device.

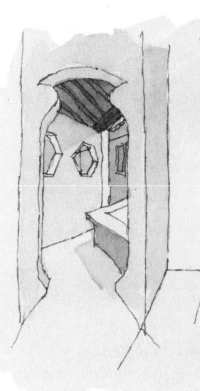

A standing stone garden of strange needle-like stones

Shanghai

Returning to the narrow streets we tried the dim sum restaurant for a meal led, or rather followed, by Wang. The restaurant did not need to advertise as the kitchens had a plate-glass window facing the street with about 20 cooks working at full steam (literally) entertaining the crowd by making dim sum portions at high speed. After a short time watching this display of dexterity I suddenly realized that the cooks were all Down's syndrome young adults. Dim sum are mouth-sized morsels, ordered by the piece from waitresses carrying stacks of bamboo trays straight from the kitchen. They were fabulous.

In the noisy restaurant we at least managed to get Wang to talk and found out what the problem was. It seems that guides normally eat in the same hotel as the visitors but in the Peace Hotel he had been refused food by the management and sent to a low grade restaurant some distance away which upset him very much, particularly as he seemed to believe that this was a devious plot engineered in some way by his Western visitors. We told him that we had had nothing to do with it and I think he was almost convinced.

Dim sum cooks in the steamy kitchen.

China Journey

The Shanghai Tumblers were well worth seeing for the balancing acts alone. I have always been an admirer of anyone who can balance a wineglass on their forehead on which there are four trays with more glasses and a few lighted oil lamps, while riding a unicycle and playing the clarinet. I also admired the courage of the couple who trained the lions to ride round the ring as pillion passengers on a noisy motorbike but I did wonder about the point of it all.

The escapologist followed the contortionist and here I experienced that moment of horror when you know that, as the only foreigner, you are going to be picked out of the audience to assist. My job was to nail a man up in a wooden crate, banging the nails into prepared holes and the only skill needed was to look as though you believed the nails were really going into the wood. It was a marvellous evening.

The Shanghai Municipal Museum was closer to my idea of an art gallery or a permanent collection than a museum. They have almost nothing which deals with the life of the ordinary man, his clothes, his home or his tools. Instead they contain a great many works of art such as carvings, bronzes, porcelain and copies of works of art — in fact there were more copies than originals. The reason for this is that it lessens the risk of robbery and damage and the originals can be kept in the vaults in Beijing.

During the Cultural Revolution, the Red Guard destroyed many of the historic monuments of Shanghai, particularly the temples. Of the 22 historic city temples which existed before the rampage, only two were not totally destroyed and they were able to be rebuilt on different sites. One of them is the Jade Buddha temple where we came across a surprisingly large number of worshippers. Carol asked Wang why there was a raised step at every doorway and he told her that it was to keep out evil demons. Without knee joints they are unable to step over the threshold — that seemed reasonable.

The 'Lokpala Stone', glares out from its case in the Shanghai Municipal Museum. His extraordinarily long left arm clutches a spear and his feet crush two devils. The devils are horned and cloven-hoofed just like those of Medieval Europe.

A sleeping monk guards the treasures of the Jade Buddha.

Temple decorations are usually made of painted clay or plaster on a wire framework. The range from simple ridge tiles through to the massive figures of Buddha. Modellers are engaged full-time to do this maintenance work.

This man, wearing his Mao hat and jacket, produced beautiful results with apparent ease. But he looked very ill.

The Jade Buddha Temple gets its name from the two white jade figures which it enshrines.

To view them, shoes have to be exchanged for straw sandals. In the subdued red light, the jade figures glow eerily.

Monks reciting prayers to the beating of a wooden gong.

China Journey

Shanghai to Suzhou

I have never seen people playing chess in a waiting room before, but it seemed appropriate in this vast domed space with its marble floor and tall case clock standing in one corner and a marble chess board in the other. This was the waiting room for the 'soft class' passengers in Shanghai railway station. What was surprising was that they were playing at seven-thirty in the morning.

The platform was all noise, steam and bustle. Attendants stood at intervals waiting for the arrival of the train which pulled up precisely where it was supposed to, every door opposite an attendant.

The table between our seats had a lace tablecloth and a small reading lamp beneath the curtained window. Within minutes the tea lady arrived wearing a blue hat with a red star on it, to serve green tea from a big steel pot. The hawkers, who paraded their wares between the seats, made a bee-line for the Japanese, to whom they made several sales, mainly of Chinese landscape paintings.

The weather grew worse turning to horizontal sleet and snow. We slowly rattled along the track through the railway yards where the sidings and sheds were littered with abandoned steam trains. Rusting hulks lay against the buffers, black against the snow-covered tracks, some without funnels or cabs, others looking as though they had been wrecked. What do they do with all this rusting iron? I suppose that one day it must be melted down to make new deisel-electric engines. But today, steam is still very much alive in China and long trains of freight clattered alongside filling the sky with black smoke and white steam, like a picture from a boy's magazine.

We relaxed in comfortable seats on the train to Suzhou, drinking endless cups of tea — the water is heated in a wood-burning stove at the end of the carriage — while a steward pulled around a large box of paintings which he tried to sell to Japanese Tourists.

China Journey

Suzhou

The name Suzhou (Soochow) means 'plentiful water'. It is a city built on water with canals forming a secondary means of getting about and moving freight as well as making the city very attractive. Many houses are whitewashed with black tiled roofs set in tree-lined streets.

I'd tried to fix the flapping sole of my shoe with glue and was not really surprised when it didn't work. It is not often that you need a cobbler while on the move, but when you do, the need is urgent and like policemen you can never find one when you need one. The double frustration was that we could remember having seen streets in which there were 20 or more cobblers sitting by the roadside with their machines waiting for business.

Eventually I found the man I needed in a passageway between two houses. I sat down, took off my shoe and sketched while he sewed it together on the machine with very thick thread. The crowd which gathered for this free show were reluctant to leave even when I had paid the bill. The repair proved to be strong but leaky.

The gardens of the city were much softer than in Shanghai. Here there were grass, trees and flowers which had been combined with water and pavilions to create relaxing spaces. Perhaps the most attractive was the Garden of the Humble Administrator where bridges linked islands like scenes from the Willow Pattern designs. Like most things in the gardens there was a story behind the name. In this case it happened that a mandarin built it in about 1550 believing that 'to lead a peaceful and calm life, to grow trees, plant vegetables and build pavilions is the happiness of a humble administrator'. Others say it comes from a line written in 290 AD referring to 'administration by the inept'. I prefer the first version.

Every building was planned and sited, not only to enhance the landscapes but to frame the most spectacular views of the landscape seen from inside. Pavilion furniture was sparse and very hard — marble seats set in ironwood frames must have been uncomfortable and cold, even with cushions. I can't imagine people lolled around much in these splendid surroundings.

Sometimes the pavilion was built simply for you to sit and look at a rock. These tall, sinister rocks were pierced by openings which made them highly valued and regarded as objects of great beauty. The best ones come from Lake T'ai and are formed by the natural action of the waves and currents. I did hear that the lake is sometimes seeded with suitable rocks by enterprising locals.

Suzhou

It is not always easy to understand what the Chinese find so attractive in these rocks, even after looking at one of the most famous — the Cloud Touching Stone. This was erected to commemorate the death of a mandarin's daughter, but there is no doubt that they worshipped many rocks in what is dubbed 'petromania'. Emperors have been known to bankrupt their treasuries to buy more rocks for their collection.

Wandering through these gardens was a delightful experience and we found that the more we understood, the more enjoyment we got from them. There were so many, each with its own special attraction. Apart from the simple enjoyment, there was the

59

Like a picture on a Willow Pattern plate, the gardens of the Zhou Zheng Yuan present a scene of great variety and interest. The name can be translated as: 'The Garden of the Humble Administrator.' Its creator was a disillusioned scholar/politician of the Ming Dynasty who retired from politics to spend 16 years designing this maze of islands and water, only to pass it on to his son who then lost it at gambling.

On the far left is the 'Pavilion of Lotus Wind Blowing from all sides', and next to it is the 'Little Rainbow Bridge' behind which lies a water courtyard and the 'Little Surging Wave Pavilion'. Passing through the 'Pavilion Leading to a New World' you find the '36 Mandarin Ducks Hall' and the 'Pavilion for Sitting Together with a Friend'.

The furniture of the
Nanmu Hall of the Liu Yuan
makes no concession to comfort or lightness

intellectual challenge of spotting where the various principles of garden design had been applied — the borrowed view; juxtaposed views; mountain ranges; clouds; forests; embodiment of legends.

Geometric paving patterns are filled with pebbles and broken pottery. I found the jar-shaped window was particularly interesting.

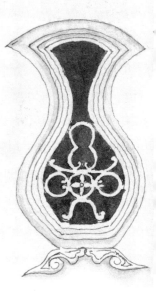

We thought about taking a boat to explore the local waterways but chose instead to watch the activity from the bridges. The canals are incredibly picturesque. They criss-cross the city at the back of the houses where at one time every owner would keep his boat tied up to the steps. Each day fresh fruit and vegetables would be rowed from the Grand Canal to join up with the small service canals which supply the houses. Today the cargoes are still carried on the Grand Canal but the jetties and steps are in disrepair as are the buildings so now they are little more than attractive shells. But people live in them and they look happy.

I suppose the reason the bridges are so high is to allow plenty of headroom for the cargo carrying boats to pass underneath, but the humpback does make life hard for the road user. We saw just how hard when five men came wearily along the road pulling a cart loaded with great logs. They were teamed like horses, each with a rope across his shoulders, dragging the heavy cart but as they reached the hump of the bridge it was all too much. Their shouting grew louder as they pulled harder, but the load slid quickly back and crashed onto the road leaving the men tied up in a tangle of ropes, their logs all over the place.

Suzhou is served by a network of small canals which eventually lead to the Grand Canal. Delapidated houses and collapsing steps line the banks.

The Grand Canal was started 1300 years ago and stretches 1800 kms. It is very picturesque.

Wuxi

When the tin mines ran out of ore some 2000 years ago, they called the town Wuxi (Wuhsi) or 'no more tin' to avoid the attention of the local warlords. This titbit of information was provided by Gao, an entertaining young man who wore his white trench coat a la Humphrey Bogart and insisted that Carol take a photo of him so that she would remember his smile!

The town's other claim to fame is that it marks the southern end of the Grand Canal. Any guide book will tell you the basic facts about how long it is, what an outstanding feat of civil engineering it is etc, and they will show you picturesque photographs of the whitewashed houses along the canal banks but they don't explain that the reality is much less attractive. When you are in a boat you can see where the industries pump their noxious waste into the canal and blacken the air with their smoke. You breathe a combination of exhaust fumes, petrol and rotting vegetables which rises from the waters. If you look beyond the picturesque facades of the houses, you realize that most of them are damp and desperately in need of repair.

A man un-
loading his lime-
barge became a
ghostly figure in
the misty rain.

Fishermen used a
net slung between
bamboo poles.

On these oily waters, trains of boats are towed by tugs, past the factories and warehouses of this industrial city. The banks are lined with parked boats and in places the waterway becomes too narrow making collision unavoidable — a sort of water-borne dodgems. It is the job of the look-out on the bow to fend off the other boats with a long bamboo pole and it is impressive to watch how well they manage without losing their balance or their temper but it looks a pretty risky kind of job.

Wuxi

There is a universal petrol engine in China. This machine has a large belt-driven flywheel and in the right hands it can produce a great deal of speed and smoke. You see them everywhere, particularly in the countryside. They are fixed to a three-wheeled contraption which transports anything from people to potatoes. I was told that its greatest virtues are that it will run on anything from petrol to rice wine and when it goes wrong, anyone can fix it.

We bought some silk from a factory whose most recent claim to fame is that it made the material for Princess Diana's wedding dress, although I found the motorcycle fire engine almost as impressive. This was a bright red monster parked outside the main entrance doors waiting for a fire. The idea is that it can get to any of the factory buildings in a matter of seconds, then it starts up the pumps and by the time the sidecar's water tanks are empty, the fire engine should have arrived.

I seem to remember from my school text books black and white pictures showing how silk worm cocoons are boiled and unwound in vast factories full of machines and women with their hair in turbans. Well, the inside of the silk factory was just like that.

At the Li garden we saw for the first time a garden which had been built comparatively recently using the ancient principles of design. There had been a great deal of effort and expense put into making it work but I did not think it was a success. We came to this conclusion after only a few minutes and it was confirmed when we saw the 'borrowed view' framed in the moon gate — a six-storey concrete hotel. It brought home to me how painstaking the work of designing the original old gardens must have been and that their success was not simply a case of following the principles. Someone had added a touch of magic to the mixture.

In the Garden of Contentment there is a marble chess board at which the Emperor used to win regularly against better, and presumably, more diplomatic opponents. It was called the 'Pent-up Fury' chessboard (I sympathize). Now it has been smashed by the Red Guards and its surface is just a pitted hunk of stone. Apparently the Guards felt, so we were told, that the only object in life should be to work. Pleasure was not the lot of the worker so anything which gave pleasure without being useful was destroyed.

In the pedestrian part of Suzhou even bicycles were banned and in one of the shops was something I had not seen for years. It was the overhead wire system for sending cash and change in steel containers at high speed (and considerable risk to those people over six foot tall) to a cashier in a kind of pulpit overlooking the shop.

Paddle boats sat on the still lake waiting for the winter to pass. The park was deserted so we made our way back to the hotel for a quiet bowl of All-Bran before catching the plane.

Nanjing

A group of young musicians playing traditional Chinese instruments in the 'Jinling Hotel'!

Nanjing

The Jinling Hotel, all 27 storeys of it, is the tallest building in China. In Nanjing (Nanking) it has become a landmark and the Chinese are justifiably proud of it. Beyond the gates stretched a queue of some hundred people waiting for their turn to tour the rooms, travel in the elevators and take tea in the revolving restaurant. Some went even further and saved up for months to spend just one night in the luxury of a hotel bed with bathroom en suite.

Every night an earnest trio of young Chinese musicians played on traditional instruments in one of the restaurants. It was the kind of music that was very easy to listen to and it never fell into the trap of sounding like muzak. But it was interesting to be in an international hotel where one could have French wine, American beer or Indian tea and feel totally insulated from the country outside – we could have been in San Francisco or London.

The Yangtze River, which flows through Nanjing, is simply gigantic and when it floods, it is very fast. It therefore acted as a barrier between Northern and Southern China until Chairman Mao ordered a road and rail bridge to be built across it, decorated with heroic figures and signs in praise of its builder. All this was completed and today it stands as one of the country's greatest engineering achievements.

Mao's bridge over the Yangtse River.

Being naturally curious we followed a crowd of Chinese tourists down a staircase leading into the bowels of the bridge. First we came to a great hall where a white statue of Mao, some 30 feet high, dominated the room. Beyond that was a lecture room where a thin woman with straight hair lectured us for half an hour on the construction of the bridge, demonstrating the important points on a model with wide sweeps of her arms. It was all in Mandarin so we did not understand a word, but we got the general drift and we joined in the mutual applause at the end.

Massive walls surround much of the city and the most imposing is the Zhonghuamen Gate, otherwise known as the Bottle Gate. It gets its name from the principle that the enemy charges in through the open gate in hot pursuit of the home side, whereupon the gate crashes down behind them and another gate closes in front so they are bottled up ready to be picked off by archers on the walls and by 3,000 soldiers hidden inside the masonry. After 600 years it is still in good condition although it was built from a mortar of lime and rice milk.

The day being Sunday we set off for the parks, first taking the precaution of organizing a picnic box and a bottle of Great Wall wine. In spite of the size of the park, it was difficult to find a good place to sit because of the loudspeakers which hammered out

Nanjing

The entrance to the Zhonghuamen Gate where invading forces were to be trapped and massacred.

martial music or Chinese opera. At last we found a reasonable spot and from our vantage point on a low rise, we were able to watch the overcrowded ferries leaving to cross the lake and the large paper and bamboo dragons left over from the celebrations of liberation.

A friendly young man came up to talk to us in sign language about anything at all. We gathered that he was one of the stars of the Nanjing soccer side, also that he was a carpenter and worked on a site for a new government office. Every few minutes, when the effort of sign language became too much, he would dash over to a group of children and show them tricks with their football. We gave him one of our sandwiches and a glass of wine. The effect of the wine was amazing. His cheeks flushed and he completely gave up sign language in favour of loud Mandarin. We parted with much slapping of backs and many handshakes.

The gnomon, the abridged armilla and the armillary sphere are some of the names of the collection of ancient astronomical instruments which stand in the grounds of the Nanjing Observatory, high in the Purple Mountains overlooking the city. These heavy bronze instruments, many taller than a man, were not treated as purely functional machines but as works of art in their own right and each one is decorated with sinuous dragons and mythical beasts.

The hills leading up to the Observatory are steep and one of the problems suffered by the Shanghai car was a marked reluctance to climb hills without boiling over. Petrol was also hard to find and we had just run out. We walked up to the Observatory while the driver filled the car from a can he carried in the boot and then

71

Paper dragon left over from the
October celebrations

The Spirit Way

took the empty can to go in search of water. As you can imagine, petrol pumps are still rare in China and I just hoped he would be able to find one before he ran out again. By the time we got back he had managed to find plenty of water so fuel was our only problem and to conserve it he switched off the engine and free-wheeled all the way down, careering from side to side on the slippery hairpin bends.

More mythical beasts line the Spirit Way leading to the tomb of the first of the Ming Emperors. Unfortunately there is little to see of the tomb except the pairs of stone animals guarding the way to the burial hill. They are most attractive. Apparently that is more than can be said for the Emperor. He was such an unattractive man that when he wanted his portrait painted there was a lack of volunteers. However, he insisted and although his court painters tried their best, two of them lost their heads before he was satisfied. That kind of art criticism has to be taken seriously.

Qixia Temple. Originally
built in A.D. 487.

Nanjing

Driving north to Qixia the fields were littered with ancient stone tablets and animals. The farmers just ploughed around them and the children in the village kindergarten played on the back of the mythical turtle, the sixth son of the Dragon King and good at carrying heavy loads. At the temple in Qixia a dozen monks padded by carrying coal in baskets hung from bamboo poles. Behind them was the temple itself which was founded 1500 years ago, an ancient carved stupa and the 1000 Buddha cliff. I spent some time sketching the cliff and the niche of the largest of the Buddhas. The low sun was beginning to set and as it dropped a single shaft of light shone through an opening in the rock illuminating the face of the image with an eerie light. The black brick of the temple was set against the soft red sandstone of the cliff face into which are cut the recesses for the

000 Buddha liff, Qixia.

Buddha images. Now most of them are headless or armless due to the violence of the Red Guards. In one niche the sculptor has carved his own likeness in working clothes and boots — but he too has lost his head. Was it Oliver Cromwell who did the same kind of thing in England?

Anyone who has seen Cantonese Opera must know that it is one of the things that only a few Westerners are ever privileged to appreciate and understand. The singing is in a high falsetto, the stories and actions are highly stylized and the audience is constantly talking, eating and moving around. The Peking Opera (or should we now call it Beijing Opera?) which we saw in Nanjing proved to be quite different and even more incomprehensible.

Group of laughing Buddhas.

77

China Journey

The drawn-out, penetrating falsetto of Chinese Opera is hard to describe. Peking Opera seemed to be more static than the Cantonese version. After 40 minutes only 2 characters had appeared — one of them 'cut' his finger to write a love letter.

Nanjing

Almost all of the audience were old men dressed in blue tunics and baggy trousers. They sat in their numbered seats and stayed there quietly, applauding only when some particularly extravagant gesture or penetrating note caught their fancy. Like the theatre, the scenery was stark — a couple of mountains projected onto the backcloth. Another and more wobbly projector explained the story in vertical titles at the side of the stage. After 45 minutes only two characters had appeared and we had lost track of the story so we decided to admit defeat and forego the rest of the scheduled four-hour performance.

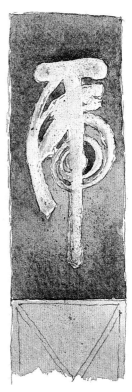

Chinese calligraphy is a mysterious art, but these examples overcome the language barrier. The battle pennant of Hong Xiuquan is a powerful piece of graphics — so is the explosive interpretation of the character for 'tiger,' painted by the Emperor Quian Long.

Photography is taken seriously in China. Black and white is the choice of amateurs. Sometimes we came across groups looking at rolls of wet negatives in the dusty streets.

The most popular pose is to f the camera wearing a solemn expression — of course there ar exceptions.

An automatic camera which produces a print in minutes.

On a Sunday afternoon in Mochou Park, the policeman dressed up in Emperor's robes and sat for his photograph. He turned down the option of sitting with a dummy dressed as the Empress.

China Journey

We were enjoying Nanjing and it was with some reluctance that we packed for the flight to Xi'an, but we need not have worried for C.A.A.C. came to our rescue by cancelling our flights for the next few days. There was no point in getting excited about the delay although our guide suggested that we should contact the local chief of the airline — he called him the Big Potato.

Instead we left the guide and took a car to Mochou Park where we left the driver to settle down for the next few hours. I think that to be a driver for China International Travel Service you need to be good at sleeping.

Scenes in the Park

Mausoleum of Dr. Sun Yat-sen.

We stood at the bottom of the daunting flight of steps leading to the concrete mausoleum of Dr Sun Yat-sen and decided we preferred to admire it from below. To pass the time we walked into the grove of cypresses and strange looking trees where a few young people were listening to a radio and a couple of girls were practising the foxtrot.

Mouchou Lake has many stories. A recent painting commemorates the day the Emperor lost the resort to one of his generals in a game of Chinese chess.

In the morning mist, the 'Chess Winning Tower' was reflected in the calm lake.

Nanjing

It was a Sunday, not that it meant very much to the workers who took their holidays on a shift basis, and it was a clear crisp day with a low mist hanging over the lake. I was sketching the Chess Winning Tower which an Emperor lost to his favourite General, when a group of youths came over to see what I was up to. I asked if I could look at one boy's Seagull camera while they flipped through the sketchbook. It was the only time I experienced any misgivings in China. I was taken by an irrational fear that he would find something in the book to take offence at and hurl it far into the lake. But he didn't and again we made more friends.

China Journey

Flying to Xi'an late at
night, we landed on a
vast sea of tarmac for
refuelling.

The wind and sub-zero
temperature made the
short walk to the shelter
of the buildings seem like
a polar trek. A sheepskin-
clad soldier watched
stoically.

Snow flurries partly
obscured the two vintage
biplanes.

Nanjing to Xi'an

Nanjing was some distance inland but now we were about to make the big leap to the west up into the mountains. A last minute panic got us to the airport at about ten in the evening where we were bundled onto the plane. Seatbelts were provided but their use seemed to be optional. Strong air hostesses shut the doors and provided us with green tea. To get their attention there was a fascinating call button which looked just like a green wine gum in the middle of a fried egg.

About halfway to Xi'an we landed for refuelling at what seemed to be a large military airport but in the dark we could see very little. It was bitterly cold. The icy wind blew the snow across the tarmac, drifting it up against the wheels of an ancient biplane complete with wheel spats and three-bladed propeller. The sentry guarding the biplane looked huge in his fur-lined greatcoat, fur hat and gloves. He pointed in the general direction of the light of the terminal building which could just be seen through the snow flurries. By the time we got inside, we had forgotten what warmth was like.

It was after midnight but that didn't seem to concern the staff of the terminal who cheerfully went about getting us plenty of green tea or delicious bowls of hot noodles. Lights were switched on in the glass showcases so that we could look at the souvenirs for sale while we waited. Then it was back to the plane for the final leg of the flight.

It was two in the morning when we dropped with a bone-shaking thump onto the runway of Xi'an (Sian) airport. We wondered what kind of problems the delays in the flight would have caused. Would the hotel room still be available, would we find transport to the hotel at this time of night? But we need not have worried, for waiting to welcome us were a new guide and driver. I felt they had gone way beyond the call of duty to turn out so late, yet they seemed less concerned by the hour than by the time we had lost to see the city. As we drove into town Chua told us what we would have seen had it not been so dark.

I must admit, the only thing I knew about the city of Xi'an was that it was the site of the Terracotta Army. I did not know that it was once the largest city in the world due to its position at the eastern end of the Silk Road or that it was the centre of many other great archaeological sites, but Chua soon put us right on that.

China Journey

Xi'an

By daylight the city appeared to be brownish grey, the colour of the local stone. There seemed to be no other colour in the low buildings.

The Emperor whose tomb we had come to see was Qin Shi Huang, the first Emperor of the Qing dynasty. His burial mound had been known about for a long time and Ming documents told of the way in which he was buried, of the rivers of mercury, of the pearl embedded ceilings, of the bronze walls and many other treasures in this necropolis. Archaeologists have carried out tests which bear out the accuracy of the documents, but it was not until some peasants were digging for a well that they came upon the standing army of 6,000 terracotta soldiers.

For me, the most exciting thing is that only a tiny fraction of the treasures have been uncovered. The attitude of the Chinese is one of incredible patience. What does it matter if it takes another 100 years to finish the job? It will be all the better for the development of improved technology.

The mound rose out of the surrounding fields. It used to be twice as high but the collapse of the chambers below and the weather have mellowed its form. Five miles away there was the hard outline of the hanger-like structure built over the site of the Terracotta Army.

Sunbeams filtered from the roof lights through the dusty air, on to the excavations. It was like a sepia movie of a First World War scene with rows of soldiers standing in deep trenches. In the front ranks were the restored figures and as one looked further back, so they became more fractured and engulfed in earth until eventually it swallowed them up. Between the trenches were the half round depressions of the roof timbers, totally rotted away.

As with so many other things we had seen, it was the scale of the work as well as the artistic content that was so impressive. Six thousand figures, each taller than a man, in this one area alone. No wonder the Emperor needed to keep 700,000 men working on it for 36 years. Like the Pharoahs of Egypt he ordered that those remaining were to be buried with him — alive.

Virtually all of the figures had been crushed by the falling roof so those we saw were the result of careful restoration. I was surprised that so many of them had a moustache, often the handlebar type, whereas today's Chinese usually sports the wispy Clark Gable or Fu Manchu variety. Each figure clutched at a weapon but the wooden shafts had rotted away long ago.

The highlight of the exhibition was undoubtedly the restored bronze horses and a chariot in which many different metals had been brought together to produce an exquisite work. Four bronze

Head of one of the excavated chariot horses.

horses with bridles inlaid with gold and silver drew a chariot of fantastic design.

After visiting the restored Terracotta Army we returned to see the restored city walls and Moslem Mosque. I began to have further misgivings about the policy of rebuilding the old into something as good as new. I can understand the logic. A new coat of paint preserves woodwork, and should the woodwork rot, it seems equally sensible to replace it. If you do this for new buildings, then why not for old, and if the building is a wooden temple built 500 years ago which has now been totally renewed and looks as if it might have been built yesterday, is that not better than letting the old castles and churches simply collapse into a picturesque heap of stone? Logical it may be, but such restoration irreplaceably destroys the patina of age so the stones of the city walls stand out clean and square against the weathered originals.

Moslems form the largest of China's minority groups and the largest of their mosques was in Xi'an. Interesting restoration work was taking place inside and it gave an insight into the care with which these projects are handled. Major roof trusses were being replaced by seasoned tree trunks shaped by an adze.

China Journey

Entrance to the Grand Mosque, Xi'an.

Even in such a major
work as the replacement of
the roof of the Great Hall of
the Grand Mosque, modern
equipment was rejected and
the massive timbers were hewn
and shaped with the ancient
adze.

Notches were then cut with saws in which the tension is
maintained by twisting a string. It looked slow work in the world
of power tools, but it was comforting that the old trusses were
being replaced by timbers fashioned in exactly the same way and
with the same tools as the originals. The restoration workers were
also painting the timbers with a mixture identical to that used
when the Mosque was first built.

The building of the Great Mosque is an interesting blend of
Chinese and Islamic architecture where even the story of its
existence is told in Arabic writing on stone stele.

China Journey

Beijing

It is not unusual for C.A.A.C and the military to help each other out when needed so we flew from Xi'an in a military aircraft surrounded by important looking military men. A couple of Americans warned us to be very careful of afflictions of the upper respiratory tract caused by the people of Beijing spitting in the streets. They told us that the best way to avoid the problem was to wear a face mask.

We didn't get the face masks but we found it was essential to buy some warmer clothes. The thick sweaters and coats we had thought so cozy in Hong Kong did little to keep out the icy winds and we were told the best place to buy them would be the Beijing Friendship Store. There is one of these giant shops in all the large towns and they are there to sell to tourists or at least, to anyone with tourist currency.

It was a bit like Harrods on the first day of the sales except that the crowd was good humoured and everyone was more intent on having a good time than actually buying anything. We seemed to be the only foreigners in the place.

In the clothes department we served ourselves from the racks of padded jackets determined to get something which would beat the cold. We finished up looking like Arctic explorers. My selection was a Chinese-made parka, stuffed with kapok until it was almost round, together with a padded hood and waterproof over-jacket. Carol really wanted something more ethnic but settled for a practical solution in the form of a long padded coat.

We were lucky enough to have friends in Beijing and they took us out for our first meal at the Sun Altar restaurant where we could talk. We hoped to get an insider's view on what would specially appeal to us on the rest of our journey but after a couple of bottles of the Great Wall wine and 13 courses, we were having such a good time that somehow we forgot to ask them.

Architectural books often refer to the Temple of Heaven as one of the great pieces of Eastern architecture. It is like a piece of sculpture, free from all practical restrictions — no toilets, no administration offices etc — just one big space devoted to art, form and decoration set in its own man-made landscape.

The circular temple lay at one end of the processional way. Its layers of tile roofs repeated the form of the plan. Inside the red lacquer columns soared into the mass of gaudy decoration, swirling gold dragons and intricate patterns. Too extreme for my taste.

The spaces made the place very mysterious. Within the formal plan of the landscape, with its straight paths and axial layout, the

The Temple of Heaven — the pinnacle of Ming architecture.

Kite flyers.

simple forms of the temples became very powerful. Ancient cypress trees contrasted with the outlines of the buildings. On the Bridge of Vermillion Stairway the old men flew complicated kites. At the far end there was a gateway comprising several arches carved to represent the clouds, beyond which lay the Circular Mound. Here, on top of the three round marble terraces, the Emperor 'spoke to the heavens'. It felt evil to me, like the eerie atmosphere of an Aztec sacrificial altar.

Some years earlier I had read of the Summer Palace, known as the Yuan Ming Yuan and built in the 1740s on the shores of Kunming Lake, by a talented Jesuit priest. Naturally he designed the buildings in the style of his native Italy and the complex soon became the favourite of the Emperors. Unfortunately, due to a dispute between the Emperor and the British Government, a punitive expedition of British and French soldiers was led by Lord Elgin to demolish the European Palaces. They didn't just destroy them, they took them apart stone by stone and while the Yuan Ming Yuan was being destroyed, the soldiers also burned down the 200 pavilions of the Summer Palace for good measure. Over the last 100 years the peasant farmers have completed the obliteration, carting away the rubble for their buildings.

Beijing

We had some trouble finding the place. No one seemed to know it, but eventually we arrived at the overgrown fields that marked the site of the palaces. A few stones now stood rescued from the bushes. They were decorated with low relief sculptures of European suits of armour, cannons, swords and other weapons of war — strange motifs for a priest to choose. Now there is a shed on the site which acts as a temporary museum. There are moves to recover the stones and rebuild some of the palaces from contemporary drawings.

The mysterious circular mound.

China Journey

A fashionably dressed couple whisper to another couple around a curved wall near the Temple of Heaven.

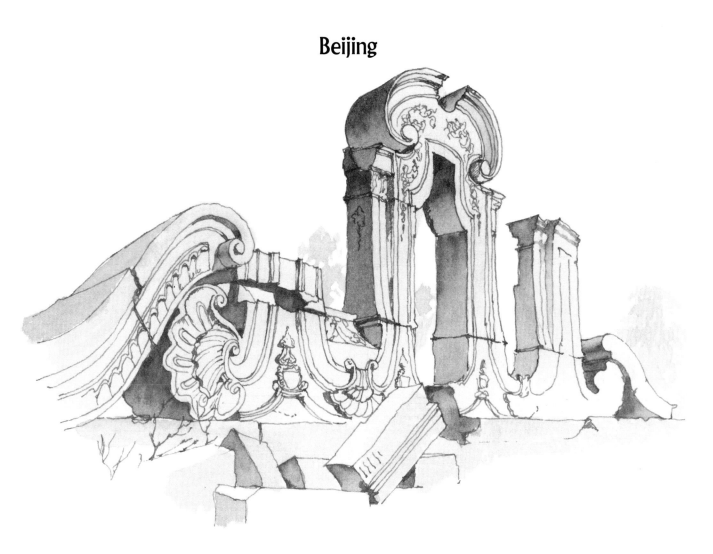

Two Jesuit Priests created the Ynanming Yuan in an Italinate style.

This fabled group of buildings was destroyed by Lord Elgin during a punitive expedition.

We saw only a few pieces of ornately carved stone to remind us of past glories.

The marble boat which the Empress built at the Navy's expense.

Beijing

The infamous Dowager
Empress Cixi was determined to
replace the destroyed palaces with
something even more grand and to do
so she raided the coffers of the Navy, using
money destined to buy ships. Her cynical
reaction to her Navy's protests was to build a
marble boat which is now 'anchored' on the lake. Nearby is the
boat which inspired it, a real Mississippi paddle boat which came
as a gift from America.

The rebuilt palace flows down the hillside to the lake. It
contained a few surprises, like distorting mirrors and the first
electric light, but personally I found that the buildings were not as
interesting as the surroundings. Kunming Lake was frozen. Dead
lilies lay captured in the ice and the rising mists in the distance
gave an air of unreality to the 17-arch bridge. Behind the palace
were the boathouses and a pretty stream over which there were
two rainbow bridges. One of them was piled with an incongruous
load of coal.

Every pavilion had a romantic name. In fact, inventing them
must have been a full-time occupation. Purple Mist from the East,
Hall of Cultivating Happiness, Facing the Seagulls, Cloud

Most bridges are arched but the one leading to the
Imperial Boathouses at the Summer Palace had a
flat centre span — it was a good spot to view the Marble Boat.

Mythical turtle at the entrance to the Valley of the Ming Tombs.

Dispelling Hall, Hall of Embroidered Clouds, and so on. Carol and I started the game of naming the rooms in our own home.

We had already seen the patient approach to excavation adopted by the Chinese archeologists at the Terracotta Warriors and now, at the Valley of the Ming Tombs, we were to see another example of it. In this valley there are 13 tombs of the Ming Emperors, each presumably containing treasures, yet we were told that only one had been excavated and opened to the public — that of the Emperor Dingling.

China Journey

Mythical Crocodile — Ding Ling Tomb.

The approach to the Valley was guarded by the statues of the Spirit Way where massive figures of mythical animals, civil servants and soldiers lined the route to the tombs. Jammed in between these ancient carvings were the hamburger stands, bus parks, drinks stands and piles of empty crates. Queues of diesel buses over the years had blackened the stonework.

The underground chambers of Dingling's tomb were almost empty. There were a few items of carved marble and some red wooden boxes representing the original contents. The side chamber, reserved for the Empress, had never had anything in it because she died during a war and there was no time for a state funeral. Although the tomb itself was a little disappointing, the treasures on display in the museum more than made up for it.

Apart from the historic treasures of Beijing there were always the everyday sights which kept our eyes open. For instance, above the shops the signboards sometimes have romanized versions of the names and because the Chinese have no need for gaps between the words, the result often looked more like a Welsh oath — BEIJINGZIDONGHUAYIBIAOSANCHANG.

Calligraphy shops have always fascinated me. They are quiet places lined with books and glass cases of brushes and inks. In the centre there is often a table where the customer is invited to take tea. The older books do not have covers and spines like Western books, but are stitched in a continuous fanfold.

I was still looking for my Chinese glasses and when I spotted a Theatre Shop, it seemed the place to try. Why it was called this I don't know because it turned out to be a kind of antique shop selling most things from porcelain and pocket watches to money

104

Calligraphy shop.

The 'Theatre Shop'
– sells antiques.

and Mandarin hats. The owner wore a hat and a pair of fingerless gloves (it was cold in the shop), offered us tea and tried to sell us beautiful ornate gowns at very high prices. I asked where he managed to find so many beautiful things. It seems that a few people still have some antiques hidden in their houses and when they need the money they sell these precious objects to shops where they are bought by tourists or traders from places like Hong Kong.

British antique shops are generally full of old furniture but the Theatre Shop had nothing in that line. In fact, we saw no antique furniture anywhere except in the palaces but we did see several places we would call second-hand or junk shops. These were piled ceiling high with plain, badly worn things. The buyers were not tourists but people buying essentials for their home.

Tien An Men had that quality which distinguished so many things in China. It was very, very big. In the distance you could see the neo-classical public buildings and at the top of the square were the red gates of the Forbidden City. Joining the column of sightseers (not a Western face to be seen) we slowly wandered through the vast courtyards of the Imperial Palace with their

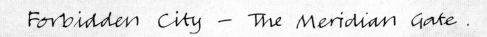
Forbidden City — The Meridian Gate.

China Journey

Entrance to the Forbidden City.

Mongolian visitor to Beijing

crimson walls and balustraded stone terraces. The further we went the more intimate became the scale. Apparently there are 9,999 rooms in the Palace but we were only allowed to peer into a few of them. Trying to see inside a darkened hall by leaning over a rope with another 50 sightseers is not to be recommended but by the time we had walked through the courtyards and the streets of the Palace, we were pleased that the other 9,990 rooms were still closed.

A young man asked if he could take our photograph. He was a teacher in a city school who spent his free time chatting to foreigners as a way of improving his English and the camera was his opening gambit. As we walked around with him, we talked of politics and education, of his ambition to be a farmer so that he could be given land by the government and become better off. In his opinion the peasants were the new wealthy class. He explained that education was not compulsory and that the brightest children went to the best schools. This surprised us as we imagined that everyone would have the same education.

One of the narrow
'streets' in the
Forbidden City.

The Great Wall

The Great Wall of China needs to be seen to be believed and fully appreciated. It is an unforgettable experience to stand on one of the heights, with a view to every point of the compass, seeing nothing but the harsh mountains unrelieved by a single tree or building. The line of the wall appears and disappears as it snakes from ridge to ridge out to the horizon.

We had caught tantalizing glimpses of the wall from the car on the journey up from Beijing. The grey stones of the wall blended in with the rocks of the scenery and in places it had fallen into a heap of rubble indistinguishable from any other pile of rocks.

The bus parks in Badaling Pass were nearly empty when we arrived. A cold wind blew through the gap in the hills as we

The Great Wall

climbed the steps up to the place at which the wall crossed the road. To the right we could see the wide slope up to the first of the watch towers; to the left the wall rose more steeply. We chose the steeper route because that way we hoped to see more.

Souvenir sellers, mostly young girls wrapped in scarves and heavy coats, stopped chatting as we passed and called out to us to buy fake old coins, plastic holdalls or T-shirts which stated: 'I been Great Wall'.

After climbing for half-an-hour there was no one to be seen. It was as if we had left the real world behind. I thought of the efforts of the million men who had laboured to build the wall on these inaccessible and barren hills. Many of them died and were buried in its masonry. Ice and snow on the steep steps made the climb down more hazardous. It was already steeper than 45 degrees and we clutched onto the iron handrail for support.

A tee-shirt seller on the Great Wall.

China Journey

Camel on the Great Wall.

Nearly at the bottom there was a long-haired camel and its keeper standing on a small plateau ready to take visitors for a short but frightening ride if they wanted. The keeper would take snapshots of the event.

I have often seen people who are able to paint well with a brush held in their teeth; invariably this has been to replace the lost use of their hands. In the stand at the bottom of the wall, a man painted traditional scenes with a mouth-held brush but mixed the paints and did the tricky bits with his hands.

The driver and guide were sitting in the comfort of the restaurant and when we returned they introduced us to a zoo keeper who was arranging for the transfer of a giant panda bear to a zoo in San Francisco. He told us fascinating tales about the habits of the panda in the wild, of the panda reserves and the poachers, and of his excitement at the prospect of looking after the bear on its journey to the States.

As we were travelling back to the city, I tried to warn the driver about the rock in the road as we were overtaking a lorry but by then he had nowhere to go. It was too late to swerve or brake so we drove straight over it hitting the sump with an ominous clang. We pulled over and got out to see the damage. A black stream of oil from the broken sump flowed down the hill until it was soaked up by the gravel at the side of the road. We were stuck.

After waiting for about an hour in the car, salvation came in the form of a bus full of singing Australians who were not sure where they had been or where they were going but who were certainly enjoying every minute of it. Three of us climbed aboard leaving the unfortunate driver to look after the car. The guide explained to us that it was the driver's job to stay all night if necessary while he reported the problem to the boss at C.I.T.S. He also thought that the cost of the repairs would be deducted from the driver's salary. This seemed cruel and I hope it didn't happen.

So while the driver passed the night on the frozen mountainside, we enjoyed the best meal of our stay in the Peking Duck Restaurant. At the next table, a group of soldiers in uniform got through endless toasts in rice wine and as the evening wore on they became more flushed and sang ever more loudly.

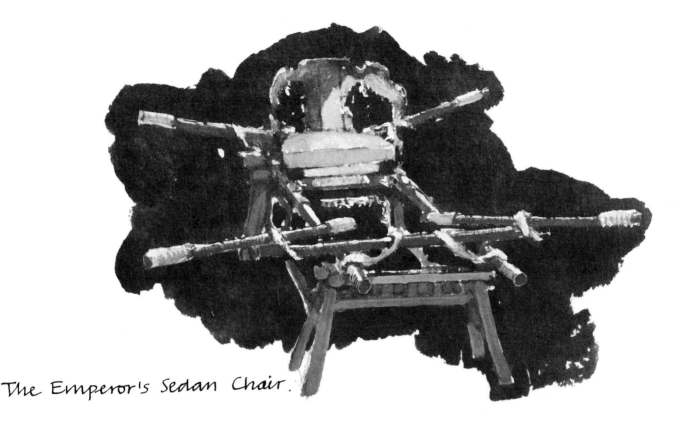

The Emperor's Sedan Chair.

Chengde

As you would expect, when the Emperor travelled to Chengde he travelled in style. Every spring, in preparation for the annual exodus from the heat of the capital, some 30,000 soldiers were sent to maintain the Emperor's private road to the resort of Chengde. Accompanied by his wives, children and other members of the Imperial Household and Guard he was carried in a swaying sedan chair on the two week journey into the mountains. Just before the Emperor's entourage arrived the soldiers laid straw and water to quieten his way and to lay the dust.

Although we didn't travel in quite the same splendour as the Emperor we were probably more comfortable and certainly got there a lot quicker. The train to Chengde was almost empty so we had no hesitation in turning off the carriage loudspeakers (there was no one to tell us it was against company regulations) and we were able to watch the passing scenery in peace and quiet.

For much of the journey the line passed through bare mountains but wherever there was land to cultivate, it had been ploughed, even the narrow valleys in the folds of the remote hills were levelled and terraced. Clusters of village houses lined the tracks, their tiled or thatched roofs supported on timber framed walls enclosing the white, square panes of the windows. They looked rather like scenes from a Japanese woodcut. Between the

118

Chengde

backs of the houses and the railway were the farmyards which housed a few pigs and chickens, thatched grain silos and the occasional stone flour mill — a simple affair which comprised of nothing more than a large flat stone around which the farmer would push a stone roller. It looked like a hard life.

We climbed slowly upwards, winding through broken sections of the Great Wall and crossing shallow rivers though we never lost sight of the mountains. We had been given permits by the military to enter the restricted area around Chengde and high on the hillsides we could see isolated sentries stamping their feet in stone sentry boxes. Their job had changed little from that of the sentries on the Great Wall 2,000 years ago.

Houses by the railway lines.

Chengde

Every scrap of level land is cultivated.

At last we arrived at the town of Chengde at the mustard-yellow railway station built during the Japanese occupation. This is one of the legacies of the 1937 Sino-Japanese war. In the marshalling yard steam trains shunted in the snow, their red wheels spinning on the slippery rails. Riding on the buffer of the moving train the brakeman let the string of wagons roll down the slope into the siding where they clattered to a halt against the station buffers.

It wasn't far from the station to Area Hotel No:6. I don't think it had always been a hotel, it had the look of a factory or perhaps a warehouse, but the main thing was that our bedroom was clean and warm even though there was no water. I was still getting used to the idea of having no door key. The long corridor leading to our room was a hive of activity where every day the staff folded up the sheets on the floor. From the landing at one end of the corridor, furnished with three bursting sofas, the stairs led down through weighted canvas curtains to the other part of the hotel where we were to eat.

The food at the hotel was plain and served in enormous quantities. At the table opposite a couple of large men sat in silence with their Chinese companions, speaking only to ask for more rice. We speculated that they might be Russian advisors.

Laundry was folded in the corridor.

The main advantage, indeed some might say the only advantage, of the Area Hotel was that it was near the entrance to the Imperial Mountain Resort so we didn't need a car to get there. As we threaded our way between the diesel trucks gathered in the hotel courtyard, I noticed that the universal method of cold-starting these trucks was to aim the flame of a blow-torch directly onto the sump and then leave it for up to 15 minutes! On our first morning we had intended to go with Ping, a diminutive girl with a sparkling personality, but it was bitterly cold and in spite of her extra scarves she was going blue so we went alone, wrapped in our Beijing padded jackets.

Near the resort entrance was the 'dismounting stone' where those visiting the palace were expected to get down from their horse or sedan chair and go through the gates on foot. Once within the walls of the Mountain Resort we were in a different world. We had left behind the industrial city for the romantic world of the Qing Emperors. It was quite unlike the Forbidden

Chengde

City, there were no gigantic courtyards or elaborate buildings, instead we strolled, completely alone, through small, snow-covered spaces and low wooden buildings. Wooden corridors acted as links and enclosures as they do in the Summer Palace, but here the decoration was spare and understated.

At the far end there was a charming building known as the Wind Soughing Through the Pines Pavilion from which we looked out on a scene from Breughel. Below on the frozen lakes were dozens of skaters dressed in their working clothes, greatcoats and scarves enjoying the day. Beyond them was the Centre of Lake Pavilion surrounded by weeping willows, some still with autumn leaves, and further away were more pavilions and pagodas. In the far distance on the tops of the hills were small viewing pagodas.

In the Imperial Mountain Resort, the Hall of Frugality and Placidity is typical of the simple architectural style.

Chengde

This scene with its beautiful variety of features appeared to be part of the natural landscape, but was not. The woods, the lake, the streams — all were placed there by the human hand, the result of careful design in which the views have been considered and the siting of each building is the result of deep thought. As the centuries have passed, the hard edges have softened and matured. It is my favourite piece of landscape design.

We walked down to the rainbow bridge where we watched men collecting water from a hole cut in the ice which they carried up the hill to pour around the roots of saplings. I have never been able to find out why they did this. From the bridge we went on to the Tower of Mists and Rains.

The Throne Room at the Resort.

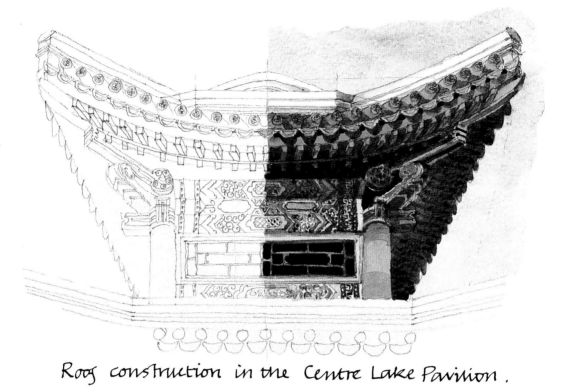

Roof construction in the Centre Lake Pavilion.

The next day we were joined by Ping who pointed out some of the things we had missed and then took us to the woods. They were full of interest. In the deserted playground a blue concrete elephant stood among the trees: steps led into its belly and emerged as a slide down its trunk. We made our way across the stream to the library. It seemed that every stone had a story attached to it. Herds of deer peered at us we stepped from stone to stone where drunken poets had floated rhymes to one another in a competition to see who could complete the lines.

The stream rose near the Golden Hill Pavilion where at one time there had been a hot spring bubbling into the lake but recently an earthquake had sealed the source and the pool was now frozen over. From the open pavilion we looked into the setting sun at a group of a dozen skaters who came the length of the lake with their arms linked. In a clearing in the trees a middle-aged woman was singing accompanied by a young man on a lute.

Tower of Mists and Rains.

China Journey

In the Children's Park stood the Elephant Slide.

Near the entrance gate a group of men were taking their cage-birds for a walk. Having found a cluster of sheltered trees in the sun they hung up the birds and squatted or leaned against the walls to talk and laugh. Nearby a woman photographer drummed up business with an unusual camera which produced two images of the same subject. Her customers would sit for a snap then move slightly to the right or left and be snapped again. The amazement on the faces of the subjects made the scene fun to watch.

Beyond the walls of the resort lay the outer monasteries. There were originally eight but the Japanese took away the bronze temple during the 1937 war and there are now seven. Their walls overlook the town and its surrounding paddyfields from their positions in the hills.

Chengde

Pagoda of the six Harmonies.

China Journey

The Tibetan architecture of the monasteries was completely different from anything we had seen before and the most interesting of them carried the imposing name of Putuozongshengmiao. This monastery, which was modelled on the Potala Palace in Lhasa, sat as a dark red mass at the top of the hill and to reach it we had to climb up a winding path through a collection of strange buildings. Some were small flat-roofed blocks mounted on bigger blocks, devoid of decoration except for the raised frame around the windows, others sprouted tall stupas. The windows were blanked off so the buildings looked blind.

Chengde

Putuozhongshengmiao — Mural and Bell.

Xumi Fushou Temple. It was built
in honour of a visiting Tibetan Lama
as a place for him to feel at home.

Chengde

Gigantic wooden Buddha (23M) at Chengde – Pu Ning Temple.

We climbed the endless dark steps leading up from the platform, emerging on the flat roof of the monastery. The walls which towered above us still bore the socket holes which had once held the roof timbers of a building long destroyed. In the middle of the roof space stood an old temple which looked neglected. Snow drifted in through open doors. The red hessian covering of the wooden columns had slid downwards like a schoolboy's socks. I was comfortable with this show of neglect and found it easy to enjoy. It was so much gentler on the eye than the painted splendour of the renovated temples.

137

Putuozhongshengmiao – On the monastery roof
there is a delapidated but attractive temple.

Chengde

In our meandering through narrow passageways, spartan rooms and small courtyards we saw no one. It was as if these monasteries and pagodas had been deserted by their human occupants and left in the care of the giant wooden Buddhas.

Once back in the hotel, I wrote a diplomatic note to the manager explaining that I had been unable to wash or shave properly since we arrived as there was no water in the taps,

Puning Temple Gateway.

The Temple of Universal Happiness is well named. It looks out at the rock known as the Emperor's Hammer and in the gloom near the roof writhing figures can be seen.

although there was plenty of very hot water in the radiators. Some time later six thermos flasks full of boiling water arrived with a message asking me to see the manager who would be waiting in the lobby. The meeting actually took place outside on the hotel entrance steps with the local China travel boss, not the manager, in front of an audience of Miss Ping and 20 lorry drivers who just happened to be there.

Chengde

The Head of China Travel explains

He addressed the audience in a loud voice explaining the problems that China had with its tourist industry and its water supply. He then launched into a speech which ranged far and wide and lasted well over 15 minutes, with pauses only for his words to be translated for me. It was clear that he was thoroughly enjoying himself. By the time he finished I was dying to get back into the warmth of the hotel, but the audience was still there and obviously waiting for my reply. I had the good sense to avoid the question of the water supply which by now had become a rather embarrassing subject. Instead I was able to publicly thank the assembled crowd for a journey on which we had seen so many strange and wonderful sights and met so many fascinating people. We all applauded each other and went inside for a cup of tea.

Xi'an
(Sian)

CHINA

Hong Kong